ASSASSINATION AND ITS AFTERMATH

HOW A PHOTOGRAPH REASSURED A SHOCKED NATION

by Don Nardo

Content Adviser: Sheila Blackford
Managing Editor, *American President*
Miller Center, University of Virginia

COMPASS POINT BOOKS
a capstone imprint

Compass Point Books are published by Capstone,
1710 Roe Crest Drive, North Mankato, Minnesota 56003
www.capstonepub.com

Managing Editor: Catherine Neitge
Designer: Tracy Davies McCabe
Media Researcher: Wanda Winch
Library Consultant: Kathleen Baxter
Production Specialist: Kathy McColley

Image Credits
AP Images: PRNewsFoto/Newseum, 9; Corbis, 26, 28, 34, 57 (top right), Corbis:
Bettmann, 29, 36; Courtesy of Cecil Stoughton's family, 57 (top left); "From *Antiques
Roadshow*, Orlando, Florida 2008," website http://www.pbs.org/wgbh/roadshow/fts/
orlando_200702A13_ss.html#18) ©1997–2013 WGBH Educational Foundation, 53,
59 (bottom); The John F. Kennedy Presidential Library and Museum, Boston, 56 (b),
The John F. Kennedy Presidential Library and Museum, Boston: Cecil Stoughton, 5,
6, 8, 10, 30, 31, 33, 46, 47, The John F. Kennedy Presidential Library and Museum,
Boston: Harold Sellers, 58 (t),The John F. Kennedy Presidential Library and Museum,
Boston: Richard Sears, 15, The John F. Kennedy Presidential Library and Museum,
Boston: Toni Frissell Collection, Library of Congress, 17; Library of Congress: Prints
and Photographs Division, 21, 25, *Dallas Times Herald*/Bob Jackson, 51, Thomas J.
O'Halloran, 57 (b); Lyndon Baines Johnson Library, 56 (t), Lyndon Baines Johnson
Library: Cecil Stoughton, cover, 13, 38, 40, 41, 43, 45, 48-49, 59 (t), Lyndon
Baines Johnson Library: Frank Muto, 14, 20, Lyndon Baines Johnson Library: Robert
Knudsen, 58 (b), Lyndon Baines Johnson Library: Yoichi Okamoto, 19, 23; Newscom:
KRT/Gary Bogdon, 54

Library of Congress Cataloging-in-Publication Data
Nardo, Don, 1947–
  Assassination and its aftermath : how a photograph reassured a shocked nation /
by Don Nardo.
      pages cm.—(Captured history)
  Includes bibliographical references and index.
  ISBN 978-0-7565-4692-2 (library binding)
  ISBN 978-0-7565-4698-4 (paperback)
  ISBN 978-0-7565-4696-0 (ebook PDF)
1. Kennedy, John F. (John Fitzgerald), 1917–1963—Assassination—Juvenile
literature. 2. Johnson, Lyndon B. (Lyndon Baines), 1908–1973—Inauguration,
1963—Juvenile literature. 3. Presidents—Succession—United States—History—
20th century—Juvenile literature. 4. Stoughton, Cecil—Juvenile literature.
5. Photojournalists—United States—History—20th century—Juvenile literature.
I. Title.
E842.9.N345 2014
973.922092—dc23   2012051716

Printed in the United States of America in North Mankato, Minnesota.
032013   007223CGF13

TABLEOFCONTENTS

ChapterOne
TRANSFER OF POWER

Cecil Stoughton was pleased to see the sun shining brightly in a cloudless Texas sky. As official White House photographer, he regularly took photos to document President John F. Kennedy's life and travels. Thanks to the sunny skies, Stoughton knew, the pictures he had taken that morning—November 22, 1963—would be sharp and clear. He had gotten most of them just after the president's plane, *Air Force One*, had landed at Dallas' Love Field. They showed "dozens of flags, hand-painted welcome signs," and "a lot of warmth," Stoughton later said. "It was just a beautiful reception, a bright, warm, sunny day and thousands of people cheering."

A few minutes later, the president and his wife, Jacqueline Kennedy, climbed into the blue Lincoln convertible they used for public appearances. Stoughton jumped into the seventh car behind the president's in the motorcade, which promptly left the airport for downtown Dallas. The photographer glanced down at his camera and saw that he had used up half the shots in his roll. Hoping to save the rest for Kennedy's luncheon speech at the Dallas Trade Mart, Stoughton took only one more picture during the trip through town. He had no way of knowing that he would soon be snapping the most important photos of his career.

The motorcade's journey through central Dallas was,

"It was just a beautiful reception, a bright, warm, sunny day and thousands of people cheering."

in a historian's words, like "driving between the walls of a canyon." The windows of the buildings forming those walls "were filled, floor after floor, building after building, with people leaning out and cheering, and on the sidewalks the crowds were eight people, ten people deep."

Crowds greeted Kennedy's motorcade on Main Street in Dallas, moments before the president was shot.

"Hey, Art,
these Texans
really know
how to
welcome a guy,
don't they?"

Stoughton was not surprised. He was used to seeing such displays of excitement and affection for the young, handsome chief executive and his widely popular wife. Clearly, even in Dallas, where Kennedy had many political foes, he also had many supporters.

Leaving the bigger buildings behind, the motorcade began to pass an open area called Dealey Plaza. Just after Stoughton's vehicle made a right turn, he heard three loud, sharp noises. He recognized them as gunshots. But he did not leap to the conclusion that they were intended to cause harm. Turning to another photographer, he said, "Hey, Art, these Texans really know how to welcome a guy, don't they?" Stoughton later recalled: "In my mind I saw a guy on the roof in a ten-gallon hat with a six-shooter— bang bang! bang bang! That's what I thought."

However, Stoughton's lighthearted mood quickly turned serious. A few seconds past 12:30 p.m., his car swung onto Elm Street, with the tall, redbrick Texas School Book Depository building looming nearby. At this point, he later recollected, "We realized something was amiss, as the cars ahead of us were gone." As his car rolled to a stop, Stoughton noticed four people—evidently the members of a family—cowering on the ground beside the road. Following his instincts, he jumped from the car, rapidly lined up a shot of them, and pressed the camera's shutter release.

It was obvious to Stoughton that these people had just witnessed something frightening. With dread growing

in the pit of his stomach, he looked around for the president's limousine. It was nowhere in sight. Leaping back into the car, he yelled to the driver, "Let's get the hell out of here!" At first no one in Stoughton's vehicle knew where the lead cars of the motorcade had gone. But soon people standing nearby pointed down the street and shouted, "He's at Parkland!"

About 15 minutes later, Stoughton was in front of Parkland Hospital. By this time he had realized that Kennedy had been badly wounded by the gunfire in Dealey Plaza. Carefully the photographer snapped two shots of Secret Service agents covering the empty, blood-soaked Lincoln convertible. Then he went inside.

THE DEADLY RIFLE SHOTS

Secret Service agent Clinton J. Hill (in dark suit and sunglasses) was directly behind the presidential car.

Photographer Cecil Stoughton said he had heard the deadly rifle shots that struck President Kennedy. Another description of the shots, from a different perspective, was given by Clinton J. Hill. He was a Secret Service agent who had been standing on a running board of the car behind the one carrying the president and his wife.

Hill appeared before the President's Commission on the Assassination of President Kennedy, commonly called the Warren Commission, in March 1964. He testified about what had happened when he heard gunshots: "The motorcade made a left hand turn from Elm Street toward an underpass ... when I heard a noise similar to a firecracker. The sound came from my right rear and I immediately moved my head in that direction. In so doing, my eyes had to cross the presidential automobile and I saw the president hunch forward and then slump to his left.

"I jumped from the follow-up car and ran toward the presidential automobile. I heard a second firecracker type noise but it had a different sound—like the sound of shooting a revolver into something hard. I saw the president slump more toward his left. I jumped onto the left rear step of the presidential automobile. Mrs. Kennedy shouted, 'They've shot his head off;' then turned and raised out of her seat as if she were reaching to her right rear toward the back of the car for something that had blown out. I forced her back into her seat and placed my body above President and Mrs. Kennedy."

The Warren Commission presented its findings to President Johnson in September, and the report was immediately made public. Although many people disagreed—and many continue to disagree even today—the commission concluded that the assassin, Lee Harvey Oswald, acted alone and was not part of a conspiracy to kill Kennedy.

It wasn't long before Stoughton caught sight of Vice President Lyndon Johnson and his wife, Lady Bird. They were "pushing through the 'out' door," the photographer later said, "and I asked, 'Where's he going?' and [someone answered] 'The president is going to Washington.' I knew then that Kennedy had expired, and I said, 'So am I.'"

Gripped by feelings of uncertainty and worry, Stoughton got a ride to the airport in a police car along with Johnson's aides. Hurrying to *Air Force One,* Stoughton climbed aboard. From a window he saw the arrival of a large bronze casket bearing President

Jacqueline Kennedy (far right) waits to board as the body of her slain husband is carried onto *Air Force One.*

The expressions on the faces of all present reflect the seriousness and historical importance of the moment.

Kennedy's body. Stoughton took several pictures of Secret Service agents loading the casket onto the plane.

Then Kennedy's press secretary for the Texas trip, Malcolm Kilduff, approached Stoughton. "Thank God you're here," Kilduff said. "The president's going to take the oath."

The photographer knew that technically Johnson was already president. A U.S. vice president becomes the chief executive the moment the president dies. So taking the oath of office is only a formality. It can happen at any time the new president feels it is convenient. Stoughton had assumed it would occur after *Air Force One* reached Washington. Kilduff made it clear, however, that Johnson wanted to be officially sworn in right there, before taking off. Moreover, as the only photographer on board the plane, Stoughton would be recording the event for posterity.

The ceremony took place at 2:38 p.m., about two hours and eight minutes after President Kennedy had been shot. Twenty-eight people—including Stoughton, Johnson and his wife, and various congressmen and presidential aides— crowded into the plane's small stateroom. Stoughton took about 20 shots, one of which became iconic. It shows Johnson with his right hand raised, while a federal judge, her face turned away from the camera, administers the oath. Johnson's wife stands to his right and Jacqueline Kennedy to his left. The expressions on the faces of all present reflect the seriousness and historical importance of the moment.

Stoughton did much more than capture a crucial, highly emotional event, however. More than anything else, his now widely familiar photo eased the pent-up tensions of the nation. Ever since the awful news of the shooting in Dallas had gone public, more than 200 million Americans had been frozen in a daze of shock and unreality. People around the globe were deeply troubled to learn that the leader of the free world had been struck down.

Everyone needed to know that the smooth and majestic transfer of power prescribed by the U.S. Constitution for such an emergency had occurred. Thanks to Cecil Stoughton's professionalism and skills, they did. As Bobbi Baker Burrows, then the director of photography for *Life* magazine, put it, "In the confusion that followed the assassination, his photograph told the world that there was a new president, and the country that it was safe."

More than anything else, his now widely familiar photo eased the pent-up tensions of the nation.

Cecil Stoughton's iconic image of Lyndon Johnson being sworn in as president of the United States on November 22, 1963

ChapterTwo
FATEFUL MOMENT

All events in history occur as outgrowths of earlier events and actions. Cecil Stoughton's production of the iconic photo of Lyndon Johnson taking the presidential oath was no exception. The picture's creation was the product of a combination of events in the lives of four men. They were Stoughton, President John F. Kennedy, Vice President Lyndon B. Johnson, and the man who assassinated Kennedy—Lee Harvey Oswald.

Vice President Lyndon Johnson and President John Kennedy

For the most part, these men's lives unfolded separately. Yet who they were and what they did over many years brought them to the same place—Dallas' Dealey Plaza—at the same time—12:30 p.m., November 22, 1963. To understand exactly how the picture came about, therefore, requires an examination of how each of the four men arrived in the same spot at a fateful moment in history.

John F. Kennedy's journey to that particular place and moment in time began when he was born, on May 29, 1917, in Brookline, Massachusetts.

The future president, John Kennedy, (top left) with his parents and siblings in 1931

The future 35th U.S. president, John Fitzgerald Kennedy, was the second son of Joseph P. Kennedy Sr. and his wife, Rose Fitzgerald Kennedy. Unlike Johnson, Stoughton, and Oswald, who all had humble beginnings, Kennedy was born into a world of wealth and privilege and a family with social influence. Joseph Kennedy Sr. was a highly successful businessman. He also had strong political connections and would serve as U.S. ambassador to Great Britain from 1938 to 1940.

Thanks to their good fortune, John Kennedy and his siblings—three brothers and five sisters—could afford to attend the best schools. Kennedy graduated from Harvard University in 1940. With America's entry into World War II looming, he joined the U.S. Navy in September 1941. He later became a patrol torpedo boat captain in the South Pacific. In August 1943 a Japanese destroyer struck his tiny vessel, PT-109, slicing it in half. Two of the patrol boat's 12 crewmen died. Because of Kennedy's valiant efforts, during which he repeatedly risked his own life, the rest made it safely to a nearby island.

Returning home as a war hero, Kennedy decided to enter politics. In 1946 he was elected to the U.S. House of Representatives and in 1952 to the U.S. Senate, where he became a popular and influential legislator. The following year he married a young woman from another wealthy family—Jacqueline Bouvier, whom most people called Jackie. The couple had three children, two of whom, Caroline and John, survived infancy. Patrick died shortly after birth.

Returning home as a war hero, Kennedy decided to enter politics.

Jacqueline Bouvier and John Kennedy were married September 12, 1953.

Partly as a result of his prominence in the Senate, Kennedy received the Democratic Party's nomination for president in 1960. He chose Lyndon Johnson as his running mate, a move that some other Democratic leaders disagreed with. They felt that Johnson represented an older, duller, and far less appealing generation of politicians. Kennedy's special assistant, Kenneth O'Donnell, told his boss: "This is the worst mistake you ever made."

In a statement that turned out to be tragically incorrect, Kennedy replied: "I'm 43 years old. I'm not going to die in office. So the vice presidency doesn't mean anything." Choosing Johnson turned out to be just one of the many events that would later lead up to and help shape Stoughton's famous photo.

Kennedy went on to defeat the Republican candidate, Richard M. Nixon, in the election. In his inaugural address January 20, 1961, Kennedy challenged Americans to help him build a better country. "Ask not what your country can do for you—ask what you can do for your country," he said.

The new president also challenged Americans to do better in the area of civil rights for black Americans, rights that he pointed out were in many ways lacking. In a speech to Congress February 28, 1963, he declared: "One hundred years ago the Emancipation Proclamation was signed by a president who believed in the equal worth and opportunity of every human being. That proclamation was only a first step. ... Through these long 100 years, while slavery has vanished, progress for the Negro has been too often blocked and delayed. Equality before the law has not always meant equal treatment and opportunity. And the harmful, wasteful and wrongful results of racial discrimination and segregation still appear in virtually every aspect of national life, in virtually every part of the nation. ... [This] is wrong."

Kennedy did not live long enough to see conditions for African-Americans significantly improve. The far-reaching

"Ask not what your country can do for you—ask what you can do for your country."

President Kennedy's brother Robert Kennedy (left) and Lyndon Johnson were bitter enemies. Historians have noted how they brought out the worst in each other.

civil rights and voting rights acts of 1964 and 1965 were instead pushed through Congress by his successor, Lyndon Johnson. In fact, Johnson brought several of Kennedy's domestic policies to fruition.

Many people close to the two men viewed this state of affairs as ironic because Johnson and Kennedy had disliked and distrusted each other. The president's younger brother and personal adviser, Robert Kennedy, known to family and colleagues as Bobby, despised Johnson even more. Among other reasons, Bobby Kennedy held a grudge for criticisms Johnson had made against their father in the 1950s. The brothers agreed on Johnson as Kennedy's running mate purely for political reasons. They calculated, quite correctly, that they could not win the election without the support of an influential southern Democrat.

Johnson (left) and Kennedy campaigned at the Texas Capitol in Austin in 1960.

The choice of Johnson for the Democratic ticket was one of the last of a long series of events that eventually placed him in both Dealey Plaza and Stoughton's legendary photo. The string of events started with Johnson's birth August 27, 1908, near Stonewall, Texas. His family was not wealthy, and he made a success of himself through a combination of intelligence and hard work.

First elected to the U.S. House of Representatives in 1937, Johnson was a big supporter of Democratic President Franklin D. Roosevelt. The New Deal, Roosevelt's legislative

A young Lyndon Johnson shakes hands with President Franklin Roosevelt in 1937. Texas Governor James Allred looks on.

remedy for the Great Depression of the 1930s, impressed and inspired Johnson. Its approach—creating large-scale social programs to help poor and unemployed people—became a hallmark of Johnson's own political philosophy. He did his best to act on it during his remaining years in the House. And he remained steadfastly progressive after his 1948 election to the U.S. Senate, where he rose through the ranks to become majority leader in 1955.

Over these many years, Johnson developed into a seasoned veteran politician. More than most of his colleagues, he came to understand how the system worked and how to get other legislators to vote with him on various issues. To this end, he employed the so-called "Johnson Treatment," described by two of his biographers:

"The Treatment could last 10 minutes or four hours. ... Its tone could be supplication, accusation, cajolery, exuberance, scorn, tears, complaint, the hint of threat. It was all of these together. It ran the gamut of human emotions. Its velocity was breathtaking, and it was all in one direction. Interjections from the target were rare. Johnson anticipated them before they could be spoken. He moved in close, his face a scant millimeter from his target, his eyes widening and narrowing, his eyebrows rising and falling. From his pockets poured clippings, memos, statistics. Mimicry, humor, and the genius of analogy made The Treatment an almost hypnotic experience and rendered the target stunned and helpless."

Johnson gives "The Treatment" to his close friend, Senator Richard Russell of Georgia.

Very few of Johnson's political associates were immune to "The Treatment" during the 1950s. But the two Kennedy brothers did prove to be immune. Partly because Johnson could not control them, he did not trust them. He especially detested Bobby. This was largely because the younger man was tough, smart, capable, and both unimpressed with Johnson and unafraid of him. Conversely, Bobby saw Johnson as an arrogant bully who took every possible opportunity to humiliate him.

Because of the bad blood between the Kennedys and Johnson, the Texas senator was at first surprised when John Kennedy asked him to run with him on the Democratic ticket. Johnson did not relish the idea of working so closely with the Kennedy brothers. But he was a very ambitious person who dearly desired to be president. So he leaned steadily closer to accepting Kennedy's offer.

To help him decide, the always shrewd and calculating Johnson ordered his staff to look up presidential statistics. He asked how many presidents had died in office. The answer was seven. But in the past 100 years, five out of 18 had died in office. To Johnson's way of thinking, that gave him more than a 20 percent chance of becoming president by taking over for a dead predecessor.

The odds were apparently good enough for the longtime senator. On the day he became vice president, a former member of Congress, Clare Boothe Luce, asked him why he had accepted the number two spot on the ticket. "Clare, I looked it up," Johnson replied. "One out of every four presidents has died in office. I'm a gamblin' man, darlin', and this is the only chance I got." As it turned out, Kennedy became the eighth U.S. chief executive to die in office.

Of course, no matter who had become vice president, the person would not have succeeded Kennedy as president in 1963 if Lee Harvey Oswald had not decided to kill the president. From an early age, Oswald, who was born in New Orleans in 1939, displayed developmental problems and character flaws that got worse as he grew

"One out of every four presidents has died in office. I'm a gamblin' man, darlin', and this is the only chance I got."

Lee Harvey Oswald posed with his rifle and *The Militant* communist newspaper a few months before Kennedy was assassinated.

older. As a child he was moody, introverted, and prone to violent outbursts. At the age of 13, for example, he caused a family crisis by allegedly threatening his half-brother's wife with a knife. Oswald also frequently skipped school. Part of why his behavior got worse instead of better was an unstable home life. His family was often on the move, and by the time he was 17, he had lived in 22 homes and attended 12 schools.

Trouble continued to plague Oswald as a young adult. After joining the U.S. Marines in 1956, he broke several

Lee Harvey Oswald met and married Marina Prusakova in Russia.

rules, including owning a handgun and challenging his sergeant to a fight. For his violations, he was demoted in rank and served time in the brig.

During and after his military service, Oswald read books about national political and economic systems. He became convinced that the capitalist system used in the United States and other Western countries was flawed. Communism was more workable, he decided, and the wave of humanity's future.

Along the way Oswald developed a strong interest in communist countries, including Cuba and the Soviet Union, where he lived for a while. But he quickly grew frustrated with life in the Soviet Union and returned to the United States in 1962, bringing with him a new Russian-born wife, Marina, and an infant daughter. In a little more than a year,

His exact motives remain unclear. Possibly he naively believed that killing Kennedy would strike a body blow to the American capitalist system and help usher in a communist society.

Oswald lived in Fort Worth and Dallas, Texas; New Orleans, Louisiana; Mexico City, Mexico; and finally Dallas again.

In October 1963 Oswald managed to find a job at the Texas School Book Depository in downtown Dallas. Not long after starting the job, he learned that President Kennedy was scheduled to visit the city. Moreover, Kennedy's motorcade would be passing right by the building in which Oswald worked.

In the days that followed, Oswald hatched his daring and perverted plan to assassinate the president. His exact motives remain unclear. Possibly he naively believed that killing Kennedy would strike a body blow to the American capitalist system and help usher in a communist society.

Shortly before noon on November 22, 1963, Oswald took up a firing position at a window on the sixth floor of the book depository. As Kennedy's motorcade went by Dealey Plaza, Oswald fired three shots from his Italian-made 6.5 mm Mannlicher-Carcano rifle, which fatally wounded the president. The shooter then left the building. He remained on the loose for about 80 minutes, at which time he was arrested.

Around 2 p.m., when the Dallas police picked up Oswald, Cecil Stoughton was in a car approaching Dallas' airport, Love Field. Stoughton's plan was to board *Air Force One* and accompany Lyndon Johnson on the return trip to Washington, D.C. The photographer did not yet know that he would be taking the most important photo of his life before the plane's departure.

A photograph taken one hour after Kennedy's assassination from the shooter's perch on the sixth floor of the Texas School Book Depository

Oswald's killing of Kennedy had forced Stoughton into a series of unexpected and harrowing actions. He had suddenly dashed from Dealey Plaza to Parkland Hospital. From there, where he had learned of one president's death, he had no less hurriedly followed a new president to the airport.

But Stoughton's journey to Dealey Plaza on that historic day had been much longer, slower, and considerably less traumatic. Born January 18, 1920, in Oskaloosa, Iowa, he spent an unremarkable childhood in the American heartland.

White House photographer Cecil Stoughton showed his camera to a nearly 3-year-old John Kennedy Jr. just days before President Kennedy was shot and killed.

He had joined the U.S. Army not long before the country entered World War II. As a soldier, he had been trained in photography, a vocation that would turn into a lifelong career.

Following the war Stoughton went to work in the public information office of the Army Signal Corps. This proved to be a fortunate choice. His boss, Major General Chester Clifton, later became a military aide to President Kennedy. Shortly after his election, Kennedy decided to hire an in-house photographer, and Clifton recommended Stoughton for the job.

MAKING THE PRESIDENT APPEAR HUMAN

President Kennedy plays with his children in the Oval Office in a 1962 Stoughton photo.

In a 2004 interview, Cecil Stoughton recalled how he had become the official White House photographer and offered his view of what made Kennedy's presidency different from those of his predecessors.

"I was working in the Public Information Office for the Army when my boss, Maj. Gen. Chester Clifton, was selected to be the military aide to President Kennedy. ... [Clifton] knew about my photographic abilities and told the President and Jackie that they would be in the public eye and needed someone in-house to capture various occasions and release the pictures to the press. ...

"Prior to JFK we had [President] Eisenhower, and there was no need for a photographer. He was about 63 years old and he didn't have the charisma and charm of President Kennedy, and he didn't have a young family that engaged the American public. So the press [was] not as interested in photographing Eisenhower. ...

"[In contrast, Kennedy] really benefited from his youth and the children factor—I mean, you never saw [earlier presidents] Hoover or Roosevelt playing on the floor with their kids. Pictures of President Kennedy bouncing the children on his knee or playing the drums with them made him appear human."

The first official White House photographer in the nation's history, Stoughton set a standard for later presidential photographers. With his cameras, he recorded the daily events of Kennedy's life, including official functions and family and personal moments.

During those years Stoughton "was on call, with a desk in the West Wing, where a buzzer connected him to the presidential secretary Evelyn Lincoln," reported *The Guardian*, a British newspaper. "She would summon him 'to rush upstairs as fast as possible' to the Oval Office, at any moment when a visiting head of state needed to be shown clasping the presidential hand."

Stoughton snapped about 12,000 photos during the roughly three years he worked in the Kennedy White House. These included many shots of John Kennedy playing with his young children and of the first lady, Jackie, entertaining visitors and friends. Stoughton was highly skilled, as well as creative, with a camera. He managed to capture the special atmosphere that pervaded the White House during the Kennedy years. Thanks to the unforeseen way that the life paths of Kennedy, Johnson, and Oswald ultimately converged with his own, Stoughton also took one of the most dramatic and recognizable photos in American history.

Stoughton snapped about 12,000 photos during the roughly three years he worked in the Kennedy White House.

Kennedy and his son, John, at the White House in October 1963

Chapter Three

A DUTY TO THE WORLD

Secret Service agents in the car behind President Kennedy's glance back after shots were fired from the Texas School Book Depository.

"Get down! Get *down*!" Secret Service agent Rufus Youngblood shouted at Vice President Lyndon Johnson. Moments earlier Youngblood had been calm but alert as he rode with Johnson in a car two vehicles behind President Kennedy's limousine in the Dallas motorcade. Then Youngblood had heard a loud, sharp sound that he feared was a gunshot. Less than a second after that, he had seen Kennedy, about 75 feet (23 meters) ahead, suddenly slump to the left. Even as he yelled for Johnson to get down, Youngblood pulled the vice president to the vehicle's floor and covered his body with his own. For the rest of his life, Johnson would vividly remember "his knees in my back and his elbows in my back."

What happened during the first few seconds after the shooting launched a sequence of incidents that led Johnson to a fateful moment in American history. Less than three hours later, he would be sworn in as the 36th U.S. president. Cecil Stoughton's immortal photo would capture that event for the ages. The exact manner in which the picture was produced can be pieced together from the recollections of those who were present, including Johnson, Kennedy's and Johnson's aides, the judge who administered the oath, and Stoughton himself.

Rufus Youngblood recalled other events directly leading to the taking of the photograph. "Stay with them—keep close!" he barked to his own driver as up ahead Kennedy's car raced away from Dealey Plaza. Still sprawled atop Johnson, Youngblood told him that

Secret Service agent Rufus Youngblood stayed close to Johnson as they left Parkland Hospital for the airport.

Kennedy must have been wounded and that they were on their way to the hospital. "All right, Rufus," Johnson replied, making a determined effort to remain calm.

Later the vice president stood in a small room at Parkland Hospital, waiting for word about Kennedy's condition. At 1:20 p.m. special assistant Kenneth O'Donnell entered and in somber tones told Johnson, "He's gone." A Secret Service agent said, "We've got to get in the air." But Johnson insisted that they wait for Jackie Kennedy and the coffin carrying her husband's body to make it safely aboard the plane.

Once on *Air Force One*, Johnson also decided it would be best for him to take the presidential oath right there, before leaving Dallas for Washington, D.C. It was clear to Johnson that a photographer would be needed to create a visual record of the swearing-in. Malcolm Kilduff began looking around. Soon, to his relief, he found that Cecil Stoughton had boarded the plane.

As Stoughton entered the small compartment in which the oath was to be administered, he found it packed with people. Because he was unusually tall and hefty, Johnson stood out. Lady Bird, who had just become the country's first lady, was there too. Among the others were three Texas congressmen—Jack Brooks, Homer Thornberry, and Albert Thomas; President Kennedy's personal secretary, Evelyn Lincoln; Dallas Police Chief Jesse Curry; Secret Service agent Roy Kellerman; and Peace Corps official Bill Moyers, who would later become one of America's most respected journalists.

Stoughton made his way through the throng to the new president's side. "Where do you want us, Cecil?" Johnson asked him. The photographer glanced around and made a quick decision. He said it would work best if he stood on a sofa that rested against one wall and the swearing-in ceremony took place directly in front of him. "I'll put the judge so I'm looking over her shoulder, Mr. President," Stoughton said.

Johnson explained that they were still waiting for Jackie Kennedy, who would be a witness to the oath-taking. His insistence that she be present had not been merely a gesture of courtesy and sympathy. A brilliant politician, Johnson knew that surrounding himself with Mrs. Kennedy, Evelyn Lincoln, and others close to the former president would be vital. It would give the public the impression that there was goodwill between his and Kennedy's camps. It would also help to make the transfer of power seem smooth and legitimate.

As Stoughton was making last-minute adjustments to his camera, one of the key figures of the ceremony entered the chamber. She was Dallas federal judge Sarah T. Hughes. Johnson had selected her, an old acquaintance

Judge Sarah T. Hughes (left) would become the first woman in history to swear in a U.S. president.

> "If his camera had failed, who knows what would have happened? It was the only proof that Johnson had been sworn in."

of his, to administer the oath. It was traditional for the person doing so to hold a Bible and for the person taking the oath to place a hand on it. But a quick search revealed that there was no Bible on *Air Force One*. Instead, someone found a Catholic missal, and, assuming the prayer book was an acceptable substitute for a Bible, handed it to Hughes.

While everyone was waiting for the last key figure—Jackie Kennedy—to arrive, Stoughton snapped his first six pictures, which showed people uneasily milling about the room. Then he switched to his favorite camera, his Hasselblad—long known informally as the "Rolls-Royce of cameras." When he tried to take a shot, however, the camera seemed to malfunction. "The first time I pushed the button," he later remembered, "it didn't work, and I almost died. I had a little connector that was loose because of all the bustling around, so I just pushed it in with my finger, and number two went off on schedule."

Although hopeful the problem had been fixed, Stoughton could not be certain. And he began to worry that his efforts to record the ceremony might not succeed. "He was under tremendous pressure," his son Jamie later said. "If his camera had failed, who knows what would have happened? It was the only proof that Johnson had been sworn in."

At that moment, Jackie Kennedy entered and the room abruptly went silent. "A hush, a hush," one witness recalled. "Every whisper stopped." Her eyes were "cast down," in Judge Hughes' words, and it was clear she

had been crying. When she reached Johnson, Stoughton suggested that she stand to his left and that Lady Bird stand to his right. Meanwhile, Kilduff kneeled down beside Judge Hughes and held up a microphone in order to capture the sounds of the ceremony.

When everyone was in place, the room once more became quiet. At 2:38 p.m. Johnson placed his hand on the missal, and Judge Hughes began administering the oath. At the same time, Stoughton started to take more photos. As he did so, he realized that, except for Johnson's and the judge's voices, the clicking of his camera shutter was the only sound that could be heard. In the historic

Lyndon Johnson solemnly took the oath of office.

exchange, Judge Hughes said the words prescribed by the Constitution, and Johnson repeated them, line by line:

> *I do solemnly swear*
>
> *That I will faithfully execute*
>
> *The office of president of the United States*
>
> *And will, to the best of my ability,*
>
> *Preserve,*
>
> *Protect,*
>
> *And defend the Constitution of the United States.*

Immediately after Johnson added the traditional words "So help me God," he lowered his right hand and, with a decidedly take-charge tone of voice, ordered,

"Now let's get airborne!" Obediently, the witnesses to the event began to disperse. Some remained on board and readied themselves for takeoff, while others left the plane. Jackie Kennedy stayed by her husband's side, sitting next to his casket during the flight to Washington.

Stoughton was among those who departed *Air Force One*. His plan was to linger in Dallas long enough to have the film processed and choose which picture to release to the public. Thinking back, he said he was then far less worried than he'd been only 10 minutes before. Opting to play it safe, he had taken four shots of the ceremony with one camera and four more with the other. That way, if the Hasselblad had malfunctioned, chances would have been good that the event had been duly documented.

In fact, as he stepped out onto the tarmac, Stoughton was clutching the audio as well as the visual documentation. Malcolm Kilduff, who was returning to Washington with the new president, had just handed the photographer the sound recording he had made. As a result, Stoughton was overtaken by a deep sense of duty to both the world and posterity. He "felt that he had been made totally responsible for history's record of this momentous event," historian Richard B. Trask wrote. "The visible continuity of the Republic had been accomplished. The government continued. And Stoughton was carrying the proof."

He "felt that he had been made totally responsible for history's record of this momentous event."

THE PHOTO IS RELEASED

On Thanksgiving Day 1963, Stoughton took a picture of Johnson signing the famous swearing-in photo.

After Cecil Stoughton snapped the iconic shot of President Johnson's swearing-in ceremony, the next steps in that photo's life were its processing and release to the public via the main news services, the Associated Press (AP) and United Press International (UPI).

Historian Richard B. Trask describes how this occurred: "Just about the time the plane [*Air Force One*] became airborne at 2:47 p.m., a press bus from Parkland arrived on the scene. The pool reporter Sid Davis, who had been aboard during the swearing-in, described the event to the other reporters who gathered around him. A nickel was flipped to see which bureau would process the undeveloped pictures. AP won the toss. After a dash to the *Dallas Morning News* Building, where the AP office was located, the film was handed over to a technician. Stoughton went into the darkroom with him.

"'Even though there was nothing I could do [he said later], I just wanted to be there when it came out.

And when he held it up to the light, I could see some images, and then I breathed. I was turning blue up to that point.' One of the [shots] of the oath-taking was chosen as the picture to [make public]. It was agreed that the photo would not be sent out until a duplicate copy had been delivered to UPI for its distribution. Both wire services gave Capt. Cecil Stoughton photo credit, and his picture was rapidly reproduced in newspapers and shown on television around the world."

Stoughton told Trask that the days after the assassination were a blur, as he took photos of the new president at work and of the slain president's funeral. "I must have been going just on nerves," he said.

Stoughton stayed at the White House for nearly two years before being transferred to the Pentagon. He retired from the Army in 1967 and then became chief still photographer for the National Park Service, retiring in 1973.

ChapterFour
AN ICON OF IMAGERY

When he watched his rolls of film being developed, Cecil Stoughton was relieved to see that his Hasselblad camera had not malfunctioned, as he had worried it might. All of the photos he had snapped with both cameras in the crowded room on *Air Force One*—about 20—had come out fine. As he examined them, he saw that, just as he remembered, eight showed the swearing-in ceremony itself. The rest showed the participants and witnesses milling about the cabin before and after the oath-taking.

All of the eight pictures taken while Judge Sarah Hughes and Lyndon Johnson were reciting the historic words were similar. In each, Johnson stood roughly in the middle of the frame, with his right hand raised and a solemn look on his face. His wife, Lady Bird, was on his right and Jackie Kennedy stood to his left. Judge Hughes' back was to the camera in all the photos.

Stoughton realized that he had to choose one of the eight shots for release to the public. And he was aware that—first impressions being lasting ones—whichever picture he picked would likely be the one that would go down in history. The problem he faced was how to determine which photo was the best of the lot. In the end, he chose the one that his trained and experienced photographer's eye told him had the most balanced composition. That one also happened to be the one that he deemed the most dramatic and moving.

Whichever picture he picked would likely be the one that would go down in history.

Witnesses to history on *Air Force One* were:

1. **Malcolm Kilduff** (press secretary)
2. **Jack Valenti** (media adviser)
3. **Sarah T. Hughes** (judge)
4. **Albert Thomas** (congressman)
5. **Lady Bird Johnson**
6. **Jesse Curry** (Dallas police chief)
7. **Lyndon B. Johnson**
8. **Evelyn Lincoln** (JFK's personal secretary)
9. **Homer Thornberry** (congressman)
10. **Roy Kellerman** (Secret Service agent)
11. **Lem Johns** (Secret Service agent)
12. **Jacqueline Kennedy**
13. **Pamela Turnure** (press secretary)
14. **Jack Brooks** (congressman)
15. **Bill Moyers** (Peace Corps deputy director)

The judgment of posterity has been that Stoughton's choice, made under highly distressing circumstances and much pressure, was sound. Historian Steven M. Gillon has called it "one of the most iconic pictures in American history."

SEARCHING FOR THE EXACT SPOT

From inside the plane, Stoughton snapped a photo of Jackie Kennedy boarding Air Force One.

It has always been known that when Lyndon Johnson took the oath, *Air Force One* was sitting on the tarmac at Dallas' Love Field. But for 47 years no one thought to mark the exact spot where the plane stood when the transfer of presidential power was photographed. Experts investigated this mystery in recent years, however, and in 2011 managed to determine the precise place where the event occurred.

The search for the historic spot began in 2010. Texas state Representative Dan Branch felt it would be appropriate to erect a marker at the airfield to commemorate the moment when one of that state's most beloved native sons took the presidential oath. The problem was that no clear record of the plane's exact location on the runway on November 22, 1963, had survived.

Fortunately, a Federal Aviation Authority employee named Noel Cook had taken photos of *Air Force One* that day from the roof of the terminal. Cook gave the film to Gary Mack, curator of The Sixth Floor Museum at Dealey Plaza. Mack in turn handed scans of the slides to architects who were working on the renovation of Love Field. One architect, Jonathan Massey, later told a local newspaper reporter how he had "crawled all over the roof with my camera and tripod, holding up [Cook's] photo to get things to match up with the way things are now."

After the plane's location was determined, the next step was "to figure out where exactly President Johnson was standing on the plane," wrote Meghan Keneally, a reporter for Britain's *Daily Mail*. "That led to conversations with the archivists in charge of the Boeing 707 used during President Kennedy's time, which is now on an Air Force base in Ohio, which [led] to hours pored over the original floor plans, and breaking down witness accounts and photos of President Johnson's swearing-in ceremony. After measuring out the tiniest details—like the 18 inches he allotted for each of the passenger rows—Mr. Massey had found the X that marked the historic spot."

Only a few hours after President Kennedy's death, the photo was released, and it moved Americans of all walks of life. It also reassured a distraught, anxious nation.

"The photographs of the ceremony," Gillon said, "which flashed into living rooms across the nation even as the presidential plane streaked toward Washington, delivered a public message that the government survived, Johnson was in charge, and the transition of power, though violent, had been smooth."

Credit for the historic image's creation, for its power, and for its immediate and lasting success must go to

both Johnson and Stoughton. On the one hand, there was the photographer's talent and skills that came into play at a pivotal historical juncture. "As with all good photojournalism," Amanda Hopkinson of *The Guardian* points out, the picture's long-term impact "hinges on the combination of the photographer's skill and vision with a significant moment in time that is impossible to recapture."

Jacqueline Kennedy is comforted by Congressman Albert Thomas after the swearing-in ceremony on *Air Force One.*

Johnson's contributions had been to pick just the right moment for the ceremony and to choose the right place for it and the most appropriate people to witness it. One of them was Jack Valenti, who had overseen news media relations during Kennedy's visit to Dallas. He later smartly observed, "LBJ understood how crucial it was to photograph the swearing-in so that the picture could be flashed around the world quickly."

In a 1997 lecture, Valenti commented on the epic event captured in the photo and its enduring importance to the country and its citizens: "Aboard *Air Force One* on that day, I watched as there occurred a unique celebration of the country's molecular roots: the peaceful transfer of the most awesome power known on this planet. In a brief oath inhabited by plain, simple words specified in the Constitution and sworn to by every president since George Washington spoke them in the birth year of the Republic, the president's power, duties, and obligations are passed, peacefully, from one national leader to the next. It is a magnificent, and perhaps even divine, continuity. I learned that while the light in the White House may flicker, the light in the White House never, never, goes out. The nation's frame is invariably firm. The nation's journey is never interrupted. The nation's spirit is always intact."

In a very real sense, then, Stoughton's picture did not become iconic over time. Rather, owing to the great significance of the event it depicted, it was instantly iconic. It captured the lofty machinery of the U.S. government in admirable action. Later it reminded people of the Kennedy assassination and where they had been when it occurred.

Certain historical events are especially dramatic and decisive. In fact, another shocking incident occurred in Dallas two days after Kennedy was murdered. Nightclub owner Jack Ruby shot and killed Lee Harvey Oswald as Oswald was being transferred from one jail to another.

"I learned that while the light in the White House may flicker, the light in the White House never, never, goes out."

Dallas Times Herald photographer Bob Jackson won a Pulitzer Prize for his dramatic photo of nightclub owner Jack Ruby shooting Lee Harvey Oswald.

The shooting was seen on live TV throughout the country. Besides the 1963 tragedy in Dallas, other examples of historical turning points include the Japanese attack on Pearl Harbor on December 7, 1941, and the terrorist attacks on New York and Washington, D.C., on September 11, 2001. Most people remember for the rest of their lives where they were and what they were doing when such monumental happenings took place. For this reason, over the years the photo of Johnson taking the presidential oath has generated flashbacks of that traumatic day in the minds of millions of Americans.

Stoughton himself was certainly aware that his best-known photo was iconic and instantly recognizable to millions of people. However, he did not immediately realize that, like other rare or special relics from the past, the picture had also acquired considerable monetary value. He found this out in 2007 when he made a guest appearance on the TV program *Antiques Roadshow.*

Francis Wahlgren, an expert hired by the show, concluded that Stoughton's personal copy of the famous image, which was signed by President Johnson, was worth $50,000.

Stoughton, who was 87 when he appeared on the show, had no intention of selling the signed photo, of course. Nor would he ever have given a thought to parting with the original negative, which he treasured. He had gone on the program mainly to publicize his connection with the picture. The vast majority of Americans had no idea

Over the years the photo of Johnson taking the presidential oath has generated flashbacks of that traumatic day in the minds of millions of Americans.

Cecil Stoughton appeared on *Antiques Roadshow* in 2007 to discuss his famous photos. By coincidence, the episode was rebroadcast on public television the night Stoughton died in 2008.

who had taken it. Although he was rarely given credit for creating what were nothing less than timeless historical artifacts, Stoughton did not complain. He told *Time* magazine in 1967, "The president knows I took them; I know I took them; my wife knows I took them. I guess that's enough credit."

When Stoughton died at age 88, his name remained a mostly obscure footnote to the eventful Kennedy and Johnson presidencies. Nevertheless, the first official White

Many of Cecil Stoughton's White House photos were gathered in a 1973 book, *The Memories—JFK, 1961–1963*.

"Stoughton framed it all for us; his legacy is our legacy."

House photographer had definitely made his mark on American culture. Half a lifetime before his death, he had produced what one of his interviewers, Harvey Sawler, calls "the most historically important photograph of his career: the swearing in of Lyndon Baines Johnson as the 36th president of the United States."

More important, Sawler points out, the image had passed the test of time and achieved an almost legendary status. "Forty-five years later, it was the singular picture chosen by editors everywhere to run alongside Stoughton's obituary in November 2008." The photo was and still is a reminder to Americans that even in the midst of a national tragedy and potential political crisis, the U.S. Constitution provides the means for a peaceful transfer of power. With his camera, Sawler says, "Stoughton framed it all for us; his legacy is our legacy."

Timeline

1908

Lyndon B. Johnson, the future 36th U.S. president, is born

1917

John F. Kennedy, who will become the 35th U.S. president, is born

1943

Kennedy's patrol torpedo boat, PT-109, is sliced in half by a Japanese warship, and Kennedy saves the lives of many of his crewmen

1952

Kennedy is elected to the U.S. Senate

1920

Cecil Stoughton, who will become America's first official White House photographer, is born

1939

Lee Harvey Oswald, who will later assassinate President Kennedy, is born

1955

Lyndon Johnson becomes majority leader of the Senate

1956

John Kennedy publishes *Profiles in Courage*, which goes on to win the Pulitzer Prize for biography; Lee Harvey Oswald enlists in the U.S. Marines

Timeline

1960

Kennedy is elected president of the United States, defeating Republican candidate Richard M. Nixon

1961–1963

As official White House photographer, Cecil Stoughton takes thousands of pictures of Kennedy and his family

1965

Johnson pushes the Voting Rights Act through Congress, allowing millions of African-Americans to vote for the first time

1973

Johnson dies of a heart attack at age 64 at his Texas ranch

1963

Oswald assassinates Kennedy in Dallas on November 22; Johnson succeeds Kennedy as president, and Stoughton photographs Johnson's swearing-in ceremony; Dallas bar owner Jack Ruby kills Oswald on November 24

1964

Johnson signs the Civil Rights Act; the Warren Commission releases its report, which concludes that Oswald was Kennedy's sole killer

2007

Stoughton appears on the popular TV show *Antiques Roadshow* and displays his iconic photo of Johnson taking the oath of office

2008

Stoughton dies at age 88

Glossary

analogy: a comparison that shows the resemblance between things in order to explain something clearly

arrogant: exaggerating one's own self worth or importance, often in an overbearing manner

cajolery: persuasion by pleasing words or actions

capitalist: supporter of an economic system in which property is owned by individuals

chief executive: in a democratic political system, the president

communism: economic system in which goods and property are owned by the government and shared in common; communist rulers limit personal freedoms to obtain their goals

exuberance: the state of joyous enthusiasm

hallmark: distinguishing feature or characteristic

harrowing: distressing

iconic: widely viewed as perfectly capturing the meaning or spirit of something or someone

introverted: shy; concerned with his or her own thoughts

ironic: seemingly inconsistent or contradictory

missal: prayer book

motorcade: group of cars or other motorized vehicles traveling together

posterity: future ages and generations

progressive: in favor of improvement, progress, and reform, especially in political or social matters

running board: a small ledge beneath the doors of a vehicle

Additional Resources

Further Reading

Gold, Susan Dudley. *Lyndon B. Johnson*.
Tarrytown, N.Y.: Marshall Cavendish Benchmark, 2009.

Harkins, Susan Sales, and William H. Harkins.
The Assassination of John F. Kennedy, 1963.
Hockessin, Del.: Mitchell Lane Publishers, 2008.

Mara, Wil. *John F. Kennedy*.
New York: Marshall Cavendish Benchmark, 2010.

Sandler, Martin W. *Kennedy Through the Lens: How Photography and Television Revealed and Shaped an Extraordinary Leader*. New York: Walker & Co., 2011.

Internet Sites

Use FactHound to find Internet sites related
to this book. All of the sites on FactHound
have been researched by our staff.

Here's all you do:
Visit *www.facthound.com*
Type in this code: 9780756546922

Critical Thinking Using the Common Core

Discuss the differences in photo technology between 1963 and now. Why would it matter that Cecil Stoughton had used up half his roll of film the morning of President Kennedy's assassination? How might things have been different if he'd had a digital camera? (Key Ideas and Details)

How does Secret Service agent Clinton Hill's account of hearing the shots that killed the president differ from Stoughton's initial reaction? What made Hill's so much more accurate? (Integration of Knowledge and Ideas)

What does iconic mean? Why is Stoughton's photo of Lyndon Johnson taking the oath considered iconic? Do you think the photograph of Jack Ruby shooting Lee Harvey Oswald is equally iconic? Use evidence to explain why or why not. (Craft and Structure)

Source Notes

Page 4, line 9: Richard B. Trask. "The Day Kennedy was Shot." *American Heritage*. November 1988. 25 Feb. 2013. http://www.americanheritage.com/content/day-kennedy-was-shot

Page 5, line 1: Robert A. Caro. *The Passage of Power*. New York: Alfred A. Knopf, 2012, p. 311.

Page 7, line 12: "The Day Kennedy was Shot."

Page 7, line 20: Ibid.

Page 8, line 3: Ibid.

Page 8, line 7: Ibid.

Page 9, line 11: *Report of the President's Commission on the Assassination of President John F. Kennedy*. Washington, D.C.: United States Government Printing Office, 1964. 25 Feb. 2013. http://www.archives.gov/research/jfk/warren-commission-report/chapter-2.html

Page 10, line 3: "The Day Kennedy was Shot."

Page 11, line 4: *The Passage of Power*, p. 333.

Page 12, line 14: Richard Pyle. "Photographer Who Took LBJ's Swearing-in Photo Dies." *USA Today*. 5 Nov. 2008. 25 Feb. 2013. http://www.usatoday.com/news/nation/2008-11-05-2548793401_x.htm

Page 17, line 8: David Pietrusza. *1960: LBJ vs. JFK vs. Nixon: The Epic Campaign that Forged Three Presidencies*. New York: Sterling, 2008, p. 202.

Page 18, line 2: Ibid.

Page 18, line 10: John F. Kennedy, Inaugural Address, 20 January 1961. John F. Kennedy Presidential Library and Museum. 25 Feb. 2013. http://www.jfklibrary.org/Asset-Viewer/BqXIEM9F4024ntFl7SVAjA.aspx

Page 18, line 15: John F. Kennedy. "Special Message to the Congress on Civil Rights February 28, 1963." The American Presidency Project. 25 Feb. 2013. http://www.presidency.ucsb.edu/ws/index.php?pid=9581

Page 22, line 16: Rowland Evans and Robert Novak. *Lyndon B. Johnson: The Exercise of Power*. New York: New American Library, 1966, p. 104.

Page 24, line 18: *The Passage of Power*, p. 115.

Page 30, line 5: Bijal P. Trivedi. "JFK's In-House Photographer on the White House Years." National Geographic Channel. 27 Feb. 2004. 25 Feb. 2013. http://news.nationalgeographic.com/news/2004/02/0227_040227_TVkennedy.html

Page 32, line 1: Amanda Hopkins. "Cecil Stoughton, Kennedy's in-house photographer, best known for capturing the swearing-in of LBJ." *The Guardian*. 19 Nov. 2008. 25 Feb. 2013. http://www.guardian.co.uk/world/2008/nov/20/photographer-obituary-cecil-stoughton

Page 35, line 1: *The Passage of Power*, p. 313.

Page 35, line 12: Ibid.

Page 35, line 25: Ibid.

Page 36, line 2: Ibid, p. 315.

Page 36, line 7: Ibid., p. 317.

Page 37, line 1: Ibid., p. 320.

Page 37, line 23: Ibid., p. 333

Page 37, line 27: "The Day Kennedy was Shot."

Page 39, line 14: Ibid.

Page 39, line 22: "Cecil Stoughton, 1920-2008: Photographer Who Took LBJ's Swearing-in Photo Dies."

Page 39, line 27: *The Passage of Power*, p. 336.

Page 41, line 3: President Lyndon B. Johnson Taking the Oath of Office. Downloadable audio file. LBJ Presidential Library. 25 Feb. 2013. http://www.lbjlib.utexas.edu/johnson/kennedy/Oath%20of%20Office/oath.htm

Page 42, line 1: *The Passage of Power*, p. 336.

Page 42, line 21: "The Day Kennedy was Shot."

Page 43, line 7: Ibid.

Page 45, line 4: Steven M. Gillon. "Taking Another Look at LBJ and the Assassination of John F. Kennedy." 25 Feb. 2013. http://www.huffingtonpost.com/steven-m-gillon/taking-another-look-at-lb_b_786252.html

Page 46, col. 2, lines 4 and 9: Meghan Keneally. "Exact Spot Where LBJ was Sworn in After JFK's Assassination with a Blood Spattered Jackie By His Side Identified After 48 Years." *Mail Online*. 15 Dec. 2011. 25 Feb. 2013. http://www.dailymail.co.uk/news/article-2064789/Spot-Lyndon-Baines-Johnson-sworn-JFK-assassination-identified-48-years.html

Page 47, line 4: "Taking Another Look at LBJ and the Assassination of John F. Kennedy."

Page 48, line 3: "Cecil Stoughton, Kennedy's in-house photographer, best known for capturing the swearing-in of LBJ."

Page 49, line 6: "Taking Another Look at LBJ and the Assassination of John F. Kennedy."

Page 50, line 3: Jack Valenti. "LBJ Lecture, April 3, 1997." 25 Feb. 2013. http://www.txstate.edu/commonexperience/pastsitearchives/2008-2009/lbjresources/lbjlectures/contentParagraph/010/document/1997-04-03-valenti.pdf

Page 53, line 4: Historical Notes: The Full Record. *Time* magazine. 24 Feb. 1967. 25 Feb. 2013. http://www.time.com/time/subscriber/article/0,33009,899410-1,00.html

Page 55, line 4: Richard Reeves. *Portrait of Camelot: A Thousand Days in the Kennedy White House*. New York: Abrams, 2010, p. 343.

Page 55, line 15: Ibid.

Select Bibliography

Blaine, Gerald et al. *The Kennedy Detail: JFK's Secret Service Agents Break Their Silence*. New York: Gallery Books, 2010.

Caro, Robert A. *The Passage of Power*. New York: Alfred A. Knopf, 2012.

Cecil Stoughton, John F. Kennedy Presidential Library and Museum. http://www.jfklibrary.org/Research/Research-Aids/Ready-Reference/Biographies-and-Profiles/Cecil-Stoughton.aspx

Cecil Stoughton, White House Photographer, Dies at 88. *The New York Times*. 6 Nov. 2008. 3 Dec. 2012. http://www.nytimes.com/2008/11/06/arts/design/06stoughton.html?_r=2&

Cronkite, Walter et al. *November 22nd and The Warren Report: The 1964 CBS News Report on The John F. Kennedy Assassination*. DVD released by PR Studios, 2010.

Evans, Rowland, and Robert Novak. *Lyndon B. Johnson: The Exercise of Power*. New York: New American Library, 1966.

Events of 1963–Year in Review. UPI.com. http://www.upi.com/Audio/Year_in_Review/Events-of-1963/12295509434394-1/

Lowe, Jacques. *JFK Remembered*. New York: Gramercy, 1998.

Lubin, David M. *Shooting Kennedy: JFK and the Culture of Images*. Berkeley: University of California Press, 2003.

Pietrusza, David. *1960: LBJ vs. JFK vs. Nixon: The Epic Campaign that Forged Three Presidencies*. New York: Union Square Press, 2008.

Posner, Gerald. *Case Closed: Lee Harvey Oswald and the Assassination of JFK*. New York: Doubleday, 1994.

Reeves, Richard. *Portrait of Camelot: A Thousand Days in the Kennedy White House*. New York: Abrams, 2010.

Report of the President's Commission on the Assassination of President John F. Kennedy. Washington, D.C.: United States Government Printing Office, 1964. 3 Oct. 2012. www.archives.gov/research/jfk/warren-commission-report/

Smith, Jeffrey K. *Rendezvous in Dallas: The Assassination of John F. Kennedy*. Seattle: CreateSpace, 2012.

Stoughton, Cecil et al. *The Memories—JFK, 1961–1963*. New York: Norton, 1973.

Trask, Richard B. "The Day Kennedy was Shot." *American Heritage*. November 1988. http://www.americanheritage.com/content/day-kennedy-was-shot

Trask, Richard B. *Pictures of the Pain: Photography and the Assassination of President Kennedy*. Danvers, Mass.: Yeoman Press, 1994.

Trivedi, Bijal P. "JFK's In-House Photographer on the White House Years." National Geographic Channel. 27 Feb. 2004. http://news.nationalgeographic.com/news/2004/02/0227_040227_TVkennedy.html

"Who Was Lee Harvey Oswald?" *Frontline*. PBS. http://www.pbs.org/wgbh/pages/frontline/shows/oswald/

Wills, Gary. "America's Nastiest Blood Feud." *The New York Review of Books*. 24 May 2012. http://www.nybooks.com/articles/archives/2012/may/24/americas-nastiest-blood-feud/?pagination=false

Index

About the Author

Historian and award-winning author Don Nardo has written many books for young people about American history. Nardo lives with his wife, Christine, in Massachusetts.